HOW WELL DO YOU KNOW YOUR PARTNER?

A Quiz Book for Couples

summersdale

HOW WELL DO YOU KNOW YOUR PARTNER?

An Hachette UK Company
www.hachette.co.uk

Summersdale Publishers Ltd
Part of Octopus Publishing Group Limited
Carmelite House
50 Victoria Embankment
LONDON
EC4Y 0DZ
UK

www.summersdale.com

Printed and bound in Malta

ISBN: 978-1-78783-248-0

Substantial discounts on bulk quantities of Summersdale books are available to corporations, professional associations and other organizations. For details contact general enquiries: telephone: +44 (0) 1243 771107 or email: enquiries@summersdale.com.

Disclaimer: the publisher does not condone or encourage any of the behaviours or scenarios that are in this book.

CONTENTS

INTRODUCTION

From their tastes and terrors to their secrets and sexual predilections, there's a lot to learn about a new partner. After a while, those bedroom preferences and childhood stories become common knowledge – or at least you think they do. This book will help you find out just how well you really know the one you love and reveal answers to all the things you never thought to ask.

There are nine scoring rounds and a bonus round (in case you're extra keen!), each requiring you to focus on different facets of your partner and your relationship. They test your memory and knowledge, and even your creative skills (so keep those paintbrushes at the ready!). At the start of each round you'll see a note on how to score it. Turn to page 115 to keep track of your scores, so you can determine the ultimate winner when you've reached the end. Before you begin, assign yourselves "Player 1" and "Player 2".

Whether you dip in and out during the ad breaks, take it on holiday, or complete the game in one marathon sitting, you're sure to be impressed by how much you know – and appalled at how much you don't! Whether you're left asking "Who is this person?!" or scoring tonnes of points, the aim of the game is to have fun, not a massive argument. Enjoy!

THEIR
FAVOURITE
THINGS

If you and your partner have identical tastes, you're sure to breeze through this section. But if, like many couples, your preferences for snacks, entertainment and bedroom antics differ somewhat, it's time to get your thinking cap on to figure out their faves.

SCORING SYSTEM

After you've finished the round, go through and check one another's answers. Receive a point for each correct answer. Whoever has the most points wins. If you don't want to see each other's answers until after you've completed the whole round, cover them with a piece of paper as you go along.

♥ ♥ ♥ ♥ ♥ ♥ ♥

Correct?
Y=1, N=0

What's your partner's favourite ice cream flavour?

Player 1: _____

Player 2: _____

What's your partner's favourite sex position?

Player 1: _____

Player 2: _____

7

Which of your family members
does your partner like the most?

Player 1: _____

Player 2: _____

What is your partner's favourite book?

Player 1: _____

Player 2: _____

What body part (of their own) does your
partner like the most?

Player 1: _____

Player 2: _____

What/who is your partner's favourite
band/solo artist?

Player 1: _____

Player 2: _____

As a child, what was your partner's favourite TV show?

Player 1: _____

Player 2: _____

What is your partner's favourite colour?

Player 1: _____

Player 2: _____

What is your partner's favourite snack food?

Player 1: _____

Player 2: _____

Where on their body does your partner most like to be kissed?

Player 1: _____

Player 2: _____

ROUND 1: THEIR FAVOURITE THINGS

At which restaurant does your partner most like to eat?

Player 1: _____

Player 2: _____

Which celebrity would your partner most like to sleep with?

Player 1: _____

Player 2: _____

What's your partner's favourite animal?

Player 1: _____

Player 2: _____

What's your partner's favourite movie?

Player 1: _____

Player 2: _____

Of the cities they've visited, which is your partner's favourite?

Player 1: _____

Player 2: _____

Who is your partner's weirdest celebrity crush?

Player 1: _____

Player 2: _____

Which comedian does your partner find the funniest?

Player 1: _____

Player 2: _____

Which sport does your partner most like to watch?

Player 1: _____

Player 2: _____

Which body part of yours does your partner find the most attractive?

Player 1: _____

Player 2: _____

What's your partner's favourite takeaway cuisine, e.g. Indian, Thai, Italian, Chinese, etc.?

Player 1: _____

Player 2: _____

Which phone app takes up most of your partner's time?

Player 1: _____

Player 2: _____

What's your partner's favourite way to work out?

Player 1: _____

Player 2: _____

What sex toy does your partner
like the most?

Player 1: _____

Player 2: _____

Who is your partner's favourite character in
[insert a TV show you both like here]?

Player 1: _____

Player 2: _____

What's your partner's favourite
chocolate bar?

Player 1: _____

Player 2: _____

What's your partner's favourite magazine?

Player 1: _____

Player 2: _____

ROUND 1: THEIR FAVOURITE THINGS

Who is your partner's favourite person to hang out with (after you, of course!)?

Player 1: _____

Player 2: _____

What's your partner's favourite breakfast cereal?

Player 1: _____

Player 2: _____

When is your partner's favourite time of day to have sex?

Player 1: _____

Player 2: _____

What is your partner's favourite season?

Player 1: _____

Player 2: _____

ROUND 2:

FIRSTS
AND
LASTS

Unless you met at preschool, chances are you weren't around for a lot of your partner's firsts, so some serious investigative work will have been in order to secure top marks in this round. Here's hoping you'll be the first and last person they play this game with!

Correct?
Y=1, N=0

What was your partner's first car?

Player 1: _____

Player 2: _____

Where did they work for their first job?

Player 1: _____

Player 2: _____

How old was your partner when they had their first kiss?

Player 1: _____

Player 2: _____

Who was it with?

Player 1: _____

Player 2: _____

Where were they when it happened?

Player 1: _____

Player 2: _____

How old was your partner when they first smoked a cigarette?

Player 1: _____

Player 2: _____

ROUND 2: FIRSTS AND LASTS

What type of animal was your partner's first pet?

Player 1: _____

Player 2: _____

What was its name?

Player 1: _____

Player 2: _____

Where was your partner's first home as a baby (name the village, town or city)?

Player 1: _____

Player 2: _____

Where did your partner last fly to?

Player 1: _____

Player 2: _____

What was the name of your partner's first girlfriend or boyfriend?

Player 1: _____

Player 2: _____

How long did they date for?

Player 1: _____

Player 2: _____

How long into your relationship did your partner first meet your parents?

Player 1: _____

Player 2: _____

At what age did your partner last live with their parents?

Player 1: _____

Player 2: _____

How old was your partner when they lost their virginity?

Player 1: _____

Player 2: _____

Who popped their cherry?

Player 1: _____

Player 2: _____

What was the last present your partner bought you?

Player 1: _____

Player 2: _____

What was the last present your partner bought you that you actually liked?

Player 1: _____

Player 2: _____

When was the last time your partner cried?

Player 1: _____

Player 2: _____

And the last time they puked?

Player 1: _____

Player 2: _____

Who got married at the last wedding your partner went to?

Player 1: _____

Player 2: _____

What was the last book your partner read?

Player 1: _____

Player 2: _____

What was the last movie your partner watched at the cinema?

Player 1: _____

Player 2: _____

At what age did your partner last get ID-ed?

Player 1: _____

Player 2: _____

Who was the last person your partner kissed that wasn't you?

Player 1: _____

Player 2: _____

When did your partner last clean the bathroom?

Player 1: _____

Player 2: _____

Who did your partner text last?

Player 1: _____

Player 2: _____

How long ago was your partner's last haircut?

Player 1: _____

Player 2: _____

What was the last thing your partner dressed as for a costume party?

Player 1: _____

Player 2: _____

If the world was ending, what would your partner's last meal be?

Player 1: _____

Player 2: _____

HAVE
THEY
EVER...?

Oh, the weird and wonderful things people get up to – especially before they settle down with that special someone and put their wild ways behind them. Here's your chance to unearth the dirt on your partner in crime and find out about all the things you never knew they'd done. Although they'll also find out all the things you wish you'd never done!

CRIME AND PUNISHMENT

Correct?
Y=1, N=0

Has your partner ever shoplifted?

Player 1: **Yes/No**

Player 2: **Yes/No**

Has your partner ever been stopped for speeding?

Player 1: **Yes/No**

Player 2: **Yes/No**

Has your partner ever driven drunk?

Player 1: **Yes/No**

Player 2: **Yes/No**

Has your partner ever taken illegal drugs?

Player 1: **Yes/No**

Player 2: **Yes/No**

Has your partner ever been arrested?

Player 1: **Yes/No**

Player 2: **Yes/No**

Has your partner ever broken in to a place or gatecrashed an event?

Player 1: **Yes/No**

Player 2: **Yes/No**

SEXY TIME

Correct?
Y=1, N=0

Has your partner ever had sex outside?

Player 1: **Yes/No**

Player 2: **Yes/No**

Has your partner ever had sex with someone whose name they didn't know?

Player 1: **Yes/No**

Player 2: **Yes/No**

Has your partner ever had sex at work?

Player 1: **Yes/No**

Player 2: **Yes/No**

Has your partner ever had sex in
a toilet cubicle?

Player 1: **Yes/No**

Player 2: **Yes/No**

Has your partner ever had a threesome?

Player 1: **Yes/No**

Player 2: **Yes/No**

Has your partner ever faked an orgasm?

Player 1: **Yes/No**

Player 2: **Yes/No**

Has your partner ever paid for sex?

Player 1: **Yes/No**

Player 2: **Yes/No**

FRIENDS AND FAMILY

Correct?
Y=1, N=0

Has your partner ever stolen from a family member?

Player 1: **Yes/No**

Player 2: **Yes/No**

Has your partner ever tried it on with one of their friends' partners?

Player 1: **Yes/No**

Player 2: **Yes/No**

Has your partner ever slept with a friend's ex?

Player 1: **Yes/No**

Player 2: **Yes/No**

Has your partner ever lied to friends about you?

Player 1: **Yes/No**

Player 2: **Yes/No**

Has your partner ever lied to their parents about you?

Player 1: **Yes/No**

Player 2: **Yes/No**

FANTASY ISLAND

Correct?
Y=1, N=0

Has your partner ever had a crush on a teacher?

Player 1: **Yes/No**

Player 2: **Yes/No**

Has your partner ever masturbated at work?

Player 1: **Yes/No**

Player 2: **Yes/No**

Has your partner ever had a sex dream about a platonic friend?

Player 1: **Yes/No**

Player 2: **Yes/No**

Has your partner ever made a sex tape?

Player 1: **Yes/No**

Player 2: **Yes/No**

Has your partner ever had phone sex?

Player 1: **Yes/No**

Player 2: **Yes/No**

Has your partner ever had a holiday romance?

Player 1: **Yes/No**

Player 2: **Yes/No**

RELATIONSHIP GURUS

Correct?
Y=1, N=0

Has your partner ever dated or had
sex with a married man/woman?

Player 1: **Yes/No**

Player 2: **Yes/No**

Has your partner ever cheated on a partner?

Player 1: **Yes/No**

Player 2: **Yes/No**

Has anyone ever cheated on your partner?

Player 1: **Yes/No**

Player 2: **Yes/No**

IGNORANCE OF YOUTH

Correct?
Y=1, N=0

Has your partner ever peed themselves in public?

Player 1: **Yes/No**

Player 2: **Yes/No**

Has your partner ever thrown up in public (for example, on the street)?

Player 1: **Yes/No**

Player 2: **Yes/No**

Has your partner ever cheated in an exam?

Player 1: **Yes/No**

Player 2: **Yes/No**

WEIRDER AND WEIRDER

Correct?
Y=1, N=0

Has your partner ever skydived?

Player 1: **Yes/No**

Player 2: **Yes/No**

Has your partner ever been in a cult?

Player 1: **Yes/No**

Player 2: **Yes/No**

Has your partner ever drunk their own pee?

Player 1: **Yes/No**

Player 2: **Yes/No**

ROUND 3: HAVE THEY EVER...?

Has your partner ever been on TV?

Player 1: **Yes/No**

Player 2: **Yes/No**

Has your partner ever done a bungee jump?

Player 1: **Yes/No**

Player 2: **Yes/No**

Has your partner ever experienced paranormal activity?

Player 1: **Yes/No**

Player 2: **Yes/No**

PREFERENTIAL
TREATMENT

The flip side of someone knowing exactly how to push your buttons and wind you up is they also know all the things you like, how to make your perfect brew and the best way to make you smile. In this chapter, use all the everyday knowledge you've absorbed from spending so much goddamn time with each other and put it to good use.

SCORING SYSTEM

For each question, choose from the options and write the corresponding letter below. After you've finished the round, go through and check one another's answers. Receive a point for each correct answer. Whoever has the most points wins.

IN THE KITCHEN

Which of the following fruits would your partner pack for lunch?

a) Banana

b) Pineapple

c) Orange

d) Berries

e) None of the above – they don't eat fruit

Player 1: [ ]   Player 2: [ ]

Correct?
Y=1, N=0

P1 [ ]

P2 [ ]

How does your partner like their eggs?

a) Fried

b) Poached

c) Scrambled

d) Boiled

e) None of the above – they don't eat eggs

Player 1: ☐   Player 2: ☐

P1 ☐

P2 ☐

And what about their steak?

a) Well done

b) Medium

c) Medium rare

d) Rare and bloody

e) None of the above – they don't eat steak

Player 1: ☐   Player 2: ☐

P1 ☐

P2 ☐

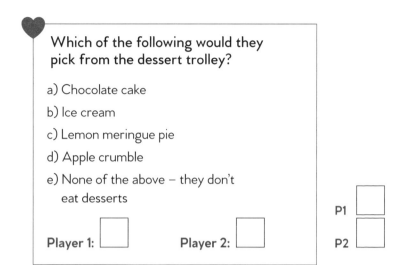

Which of the following would they pick from the dessert trolley?

a) Chocolate cake

b) Ice cream

c) Lemon meringue pie

d) Apple crumble

e) None of the above – they don't eat desserts

Player 1: ⬚   **Player 2:** ⬚   **P1** ⬚ **P2** ⬚

THAT'S ENTERTAINMENT

Correct?
Y=1, N=0

Of the following, what is your partner's go-to TV genre?

a) Sports

b) Reality TV

c) Drama

d) Comedy

e) None of the above – my partner doesn't watch TV

Player 1: ☐   Player 2: ☐

P1 ☐
P2 ☐

Where would they most like to see their favourite band/artist perform?

a) On TV, from the comfort of the sofa

b) At an intimate venue with only a few other people

c) In a huge stadium

d) At a festival with all their friends

e) None of the above – my partner's not that into music

Player 1: ☐   Player 2: ☐

P1 ☐
P2 ☐

Which of the following would your partner laugh at the most?

a) YouTube stunt videos where people hurt themselves for laughs

b) Cat videos (replace cat with goat if appropriate)

c) Amateur comedians performing in a small open-mic event

d) A famous headliner comedian at a huge venue

e) You

Player 1: ☐   Player 2: ☐   P1 ☐
                                        P2 ☐

Which of the following should you never buy them tickets for?

a) A musical

b) A day at the races

c) An art gallery opening

d) A football match

e) A big pop concert

Player 1: ☐   Player 2: ☐   P1 ☐
                                        P2 ☐

GETTING THERE

Correct?
Y=1, N=0

What's your partner's preferred position in the car for a long journey?

a) In the driver's seat

b) Passenger seat, so they can navigate

c) Passenger seat, so they can decide on the music

d) In the back, sprawled out asleep

e) None of the above – they don't like road trips

Player 1: ☐   Player 2: ☐

P1 ☐
P2 ☐

If they book the flights, where will your seats be?

a) In first class – only the best for my partner

b) Where there's most leg room

c) By the window – they like to see out

d) Near the toilet – they always need to get up

e) Away from each other – they left it till the last minute

Player 1: ☐   Player 2: ☐

P1 ☐
P2 ☐

How long will your partner walk for before getting grumpy?

a) From the front door to the taxi

b) 15 minutes

c) 1 hour

d) A few hours

e) All day – they're a walking machine

Player 1: ☐   **Player 2:** ☐

P1 ☐
P2 ☐

If they were on a train, how would your partner occupy themselves?

a) Staring out the window in quiet contemplation

b) Talking loudly at you while you try to read

c) Reading a good book/magazine or looking at their phone

d) Listening to music/podcasts or watching videos

e) Fidgeting and whining until you entertain them

Player 1: ☐   **Player 2:** ☐

P1 ☐
P2 ☐

DAYS OUT

Correct?
Y=1, N=0

At the fair, which ride does your partner head to first?

a) The Ferris wheel for a romantic ride

b) The bumper cars to be competitive

c) The rifle-shooting game to show off

d) The log flume for a laugh

e) The food truck – they're all about the snacks

Player 1: ⬜   Player 2: ⬜

P1 ⬜
P2 ⬜

Where would your partner prefer to swim?

a) In the sea

b) In a lake

c) In a private infinity pool

d) At the local swimming pool

e) None of the above – my partner doesn't swim

Player 1: ⬜   Player 2: ⬜

P1 ⬜
P2 ⬜

Which cultural institution would your partner choose to visit?

a) A museum

b) An art gallery

c) A library

d) An historic building, e.g. a castle or the residence of someone famous

e) None of the above – they aren't one for culture

Player 1: ☐   Player 2: ☐

P1 ☐
P2 ☐

Of the following date activities, which would they enjoy the most?

a) Rock climbing

b) Bowling

c) Spa day

d) River cruise

e) Cinema

Player 1: ☐   Player 2: ☐

P1 ☐
P2 ☐

AT THE MOVIES

Correct?
Y=1, N=0

What is your partner's cinema snack of choice?

a) Popcorn

b) Chocolate

c) Nachos

d) Hotdog

e) None of the above – they think cinema snacks are too expensive

Player 1: ☐   Player 2: ☐

P1 ☐
P2 ☐

In the cinema, where do they like to sit?

a) Near the front

b) In the middle

c) On the side

d) At the back

e) Anywhere, they're not fussed

Player 1: ☐   Player 2: ☐

P1 ☐
P2 ☐

Of the following, what movie genre would they be most likely to choose?

a) Side-splitting comedy

b) Action-packed blockbuster

c) Tear-jerking drama

d) Knee-knocking horror

e) Mind-bending sci-fi

Player 1: ☐   Player 2: ☐

P1 ☐
P2 ☐

Which of the following annoying cinema behaviours are they most likely to exhibit during a movie?

a) Loud eating

b) Talking

c) Getting up to go to the toilet

d) Looking at their phone

e) All of the above

Player 1: ☐   Player 2: ☐

P1 ☐
P2 ☐

DRINKING TIME

Correct?
Y=1, N=0

How does your partner take their tea?

a) Strong, no sugar

b) Strong, with sugar

c) Weak, no sugar

d) Weak, with sugar

e) None of the above – my partner
   doesn't drink tea

Player 1: ☐   Player 2: ☐

P1 ☐
P2 ☐

And how about their coffee?

a) Strong, no sugar

b) Strong, with sugar

c) Weak, no sugar

d) Weak, with sugar

e) None of the above – my partner doesn't
   drink coffee

Player 1: ☐   Player 2: ☐

P1 ☐
P2 ☐

What's their drink of choice at the bar?

a) Wine

b) Beer/cider

c) Spirit and a mixer

d) Shots

e) Non-alcoholic drink

Player 1: ☐   Player 2: ☐   P1 ☐   P2 ☐

Of the following cocktails, which would they choose?

a) Mojito

b) Margarita

c) Long Island iced tea

d) Cosmopolitan

e) None – my partner doesn't drink cocktails

Player 1: ☐   Player 2: ☐   P1 ☐   P2 ☐

HOLIDAY HABITS

Correct?
Y=1, N=0

Where would your partner prefer to stay on holiday?

a) A fancy boutique hotel

b) A big chain hotel

c) In a self-catered apartment

d) At a cheap hostel

e) In a tent

Player 1: ☐   Player 2: ☐

P1 ☐
P2 ☐

On holiday, how do they like to spend their days?

a) Relaxing by the pool, reading a good book

b) Seeing all the famous sights in a big tour group

c) Seeing lesser-known sights that they've spent months researching

d) Hiking and adventuring in the countryside

e) Living like the locals (shopping, having coffee, meeting friends)

Player 1: ☐   Player 2: ☐

P1 ☐
P2 ☐

Does your partner try to speak the language?

a) Yes, they always learn the basics before they go

b) Yes, they buy a phrasebook and refer to it as and when they need to

c) Yes, but no one understands what they are saying

d) No, they expect you to do all the talking

e) No, they talk loudly in their native language and wave their arms

Player 1: ☐   Player 2: ☐

P1 ☐

P2 ☐

What would they order off the menu abroad?

a) Whatever the waiter recommends – they like to be surprised

b) Something unusual they've never tried before

c) A local speciality they know they'll enjoy

d) Meat with chips – they're not very adventurous

e) They try to locate the nearest McDonald's

Player 1: ☐   Player 2: ☐

P1 ☐

P2 ☐

BEDTIME ROUTINE

Correct?
Y=1, N=0

What does your partner wear to bed?

a) Nothing

b) Underwear

c) Sexy pyjamas

d) Cosy pyjamas

e) Sweats and a pullover, and socks
   too probably

P1

P2

Player 1: ☐   **Player 2:** ☐

Any pre-lights-out activities?

a) They like to read

b) They're usually on their phone

c) They watch TV till they fall asleep

d) They talk, a lot

e) None – they're normally asleep as
   soon as their head hits the pillow

P1

P2

Player 1: ☐   **Player 2:** ☐

How many pillows do they like?

a) None

b) One

c) Two

d) More than two

e) They use me as a pillow

Player 1: ☐   **Player 2:** ☐

P1 ☐
P2 ☐

Which position do they fall asleep in?

a) On their back

b) On their front

c) On their left side

d) On their right side

e) I wouldn't know – I'm always asleep
    before them

Player 1: ☐   **Player 2:** ☐

P1 ☐
P2 ☐

FUTURE PLANS

What would your partner most like to have?

a) A beautiful house

b) A fancy car

c) A pet

d) A successful business

e) An amazing wardrobe

Player 1: ☐   Player 2: ☐

Correct?
Y=1, N=0

P1 ☐

P2 ☐

Which of the following would your partner most like to live in?

a) A plush city apartment

b) A sprawling country house

c) A cosy cottage

d) A rustic canal boat

e) A trendy beach shack

Player 1: ☐   Player 2: ☐

P1 ☐

P2 ☐

What would be your partner's dream job?

a) Famous entertainer

b) Prime minister/president

c) Famous athlete

d) Millionaire entrepreneur

e) YouTube celebrity

Player 1: ☐   **Player 2:** ☐

P1 ☐
P2 ☐

SEXY TIME

Correct?
Y=1, N=0

Where does your partner most like to have sex?

a) In the bed

b) In the shower

c) In a hotel

d) In the car

e) Out and about

Player 1: ☐   **Player 2:** ☐

P1 ☐
P2 ☐

What time of day do they most want to get it on?

a) First thing in the morning, while you're still half asleep

b) After a workout while you're already sweaty

c) As soon as they're home from work – they're all over you

d) Any time they've had a drink

e) Last thing at night

Player 1: ☐   **Player 2:** ☐

P1 ☐
P2 ☐

Which of the following sexy role-play scenarios would appeal to them most?

a) Housewife/husband and sexy plumber

b) Employee and boss

c) Police officer and villain

d) Medieval mischief (think Robin Hood and Maid Marion)

e) Cowboys and/or girls

Player 1: **Player 2:** P1

P2

Which of the following would your partner most like to try (or, if they've tried them all, which have they enjoyed the most)?

a) S&M

b) Vibrator

c) A sex swing

d) A threesome

e) Nipple clamps

Player 1: **Player 2:** P1

P2

KNOWING ME, KNOWING YOU

You and your partner have your strengths and weaknesses, your skills and, well, lack of skills. And that's probably why you work so well together. But while it's easy to know who's top dog when it comes to some things, other talents and traits are up for debate.

SCORING SYSTEM

For each question, answer "Me" or "You". Switch players for each section (note: it says Player 1 or Player 2 at the top of each to keep track). After your partner has answered a section, give them a point for each answer where you agree with their choice. At the end of the round, whoever has the most points wins.

PLAYER 1

Correct?
Y=1, N=0

Who is most likely to...	Answer: "Me" or "You"	
Do the laundry?	_____	
Do the dirty?	_____	
Make a move?	_____	
Make the bed?	_____	
Pay attention?	_____	

Total score

PLAYER 2

Who is best at...	Answer: "Me" or "You"	
Going solo?	_____	☐
Selfies?	_____	☐
Stripping?	_____	☐
Sulking?	_____	☐
Snuggling?	_____	☐

Total score ☐

PLAYER 1

Who would win at...	Answer: "Me" or "You"	
Video games?	_____	☐
Board games?	_____	☐
A running race?	_____	☐
Arm wrestling?	_____	☐
Burping?	_____	☐

Total score ☐

PLAYER 2

Who would most likely appear in...	Answer: "Me" or "You"	
A talent contest?	_____	☐
A cookery competition?	_____	☐
A quiz show?	_____	☐
A reality show?	_____	☐
An extreme obstacle course?	_____	☐

Total score ☐

PLAYER 1

Who has...	Answer: "Me" or "You"	
Slept with the most people?	_____	☐
Read the most books?	_____	☐
Cried at the most movies?	_____	☐
Bought the most clothes?	_____	☐
Ended the most relationships?	_____	☐

Total score ☐

PLAYER 2

Which of you is most likely to do the following...	Answer: "Me" or "You"	
Skydive	_____	☐
Swim with sharks	_____	☐
Put it all on black	_____	☐
Quit their job and go travelling	_____	☐
Join the circus	_____	☐

Total score ☐

PLAYER 1

Which of you would make the best...	Answer: "Me" or "You"	
Pole dancer?	_____	☐
Firefighter?	_____	☐
Brain surgeon?	_____	☐
School teacher?	_____	☐
Politician?	_____	☐

Total score ☐

PLAYER 2

Who do you think would teach your children...	Answer: "Me" or "You"	
Right from wrong?	_____	☐
How to dance?	_____	☐
Good manners?	_____	☐
Self-belief?	_____	☐
Farting?	_____	☐

Total score ☐

PLAYER 1

Who do you think has the best...	Answer: "Me" or "You"	
Nose?	_____	☐
Butt?	_____	☐
Teeth?	_____	☐
Hair?	_____	☐
Belly button?	_____	☐

Total score ☐

PLAYER 2

Who has the best...	Answer: "Me" or "You"	
Chat-up lines?	_____	☐
Taste in music?	_____	☐
Jokes?	_____	☐
Friends?	_____	☐
Social media presence?	_____	☐

Total score ☐

GETTING

DESCRIPTIVE

From their dreamy eyes and seductive smile to that weird habit they have that nobody else knows about, you've probably got a lot to say about each other's looks, personality traits and future autobiography titles. Now it's time to put all those words to good use and score yourself some points.

?

SCORING SYSTEM

For each question, write your answers in the space provided. At the end of the round, score your partner out of five for their answer (one being low and five being high). It's up to you to decide on your marking criteria, but if it makes you laugh or is particularly inventive, we suggest giving it a high score. Tot up your points, and whoever has the most at the end of the round wins. If you don't want to see each other's answers until after you've completed the whole chapter, cover them with a piece of paper as you go along.

IN THREE WORDS

Describe your partner's feet:

Player 1: _____ _____ _____ ☐ /5

Player 2: _____ _____ _____ ☐ /5

Describe your partner's kisses:

Player 1: _____ _____ _____ ☐ /5

Player 2: _____ _____ _____ ☐ /5

Describe your partner's kitchen skills:

Player 1: _____ _____ _____   /5

Player 2: _____ _____ _____   /5

Describe your partner's dress sense:

Player 1: _____ _____ _____   /5

Player 2: _____ _____ _____   /5

Describe your partner's butt:

Player 1: _____ _____ _____   /5

Player 2: _____ _____ _____   /5

Describe your partner's sex noises:

Player 1: _____ _____ _____   /5

Player 2: _____ _____ _____   /5

IF THERE WAS A BOOK ABOUT YOUR RELATIONSHIP...

What would the title be for the chapter about your partner's life before they met you?

Player 1: _____ /5

Player 2: _____ /5

What would the title be for the chapter about how you met?

Player 1: _____ /5

Player 2: _____ /5

What would the title be for the chapter about your life now?

Player 1: _____ /5

Player 2: _____ /5

DEVIL'S IN THE DETAIL

What was your partner wearing the
first time you saw them?

Player 1: _____ ☐ /5

Player 2: _____ ☐ /5

What was the first thing your partner
said to you?

Player 1: _____ ☐ /5

Player 2: _____ ☐ /5

Where were you the first time you kissed?

Player 1: _____ ☐ /5

Player 2: _____ ☐ /5

WHICH THREE ITEMS...

Could your partner not live without
on a desert island?

Player 1: _____ _____ _____   ☐ /5

Player 2: _____ _____ _____   ☐ /5

Could your partner not live without
at the gym?

Player 1: _____ _____ _____   ☐ /5

Player 2: _____ _____ _____   ☐ /5

Could your partner not live without
during the zombie apocalypse?

Player 1: _____ _____ _____   ☐ /5

Player 2: _____ _____ _____   ☐ /5

IF YOUR PARTNER HAD...

Their own perfume, what would it be called?

Player 1: _____ ⬜ /5

Player 2: _____ ⬜ /5

A one-man/-woman band, what would it be called?

Player 1: _____ ⬜ /5

Player 2: _____ ⬜ /5

A fad exercise class, what would it be called?

Player 1: _____ ⬜ /5

Player 2: _____ ⬜ /5

WONDERFULLY WEIRD

Describe your partner's weirdest habit:

Player 1: _____ ⬜ /5

Player 2: _____ ⬜ /5

Describe your partner's weirdest routine:

Player 1: _____ ⬜ /5

Player 2: _____ ⬜ /5

Describe your partner's weirdest outfit:

Player 1: _____ ⬜ /5

Player 2: _____ ⬜ /5

IF MUSIC BE THE FOOD OF LOVE...

Which song best sums up how you felt when you first met your partner?

Player 1: _____ ☐ /5

Player 2: _____ ☐ /5

Which song best sums up how you felt when you first saw your partner dance?

Player 1: _____ ☐ /5

Player 2: _____ ☐ /5

Which song best sums up how you felt when you first had sex with your partner?

Player 1: _____ ☐ /5

Player 2: _____ ☐ /5

WHAT'S YOUR PARTNER'S BIGGEST...

Secret?

Player 1: _____ ☐ /5

Player 2: _____ ☐ /5

Fear?

Player 1: _____ ☐ /5

Player 2: _____ ☐ /5

Ambition?

Player 1: _____ ☐ /5

Player 2: _____ ☐ /5

Annoyance?

Player 1: _____ ☐ /5

Player 2: _____ ☐ /5

FILL IN THE BLANKS

If my partner married a celebrity,
it would probably be _____.

Player 1: _____ /5

Player 2: _____ /5

If my partner bought a car, it would
probably be a _____.

Player 1: _____ /5

Player 2: _____ /5

If my partner could have dinner
with a famous dead person, it
would be _____.

Player 1: _____ /5

Player 2: _____ /5

My partner likes to think they're
_____, but they're not.

Player 1: _____ ☐ /5

Player 2: _____ ☐ /5

If my partner won the lottery, the first
thing they'd buy would be _____.

Player 1: _____ ☐ /5

Player 2: _____ ☐ /5

After my partner and I first kissed,
I couldn't stop thinking _____.

Player 1: _____ ☐ /5

Player 2: _____ ☐ /5

After my partner and I first had sex,
the first thing I thought was _____.

Player 1: _____ ☐ /5

Player 2: _____ ☐ /5

TESTING
TIME

If you're in each other's pockets most of the time, you probably think you've got a good handle on your partner's schedule. You're sure you know how often they perform daily tasks. And you definitely remember the last time they took a selfie. If you've been watching their every move like a social media stalker, you should ace this time-testing round.

SCORING SYSTEM

For each question, put a tick in the column that most closely matches your answer. Switch players for each page (note: it says Player 1 or Player 2 at the top of each to keep track). After your partner has answered a page, give them a point for each answer where their choice is correct. At the end of the round, whoever has the most points wins.

PLAYER 1

How often does your partner...

	More than twice a day	Twice a day	Once a day	Every other day	Once a week	Correct? Y=1 N=0
Shower?						
Brush their teeth?						
Take a dump?						
Look in the mirror?						

Total score

PLAYER 2

How often does your partner...

	More than twice a day	Twice a day	Once a day	Every other day	Once a week	Correct? Y=1 N=0
Make a cup of tea/coffee?						
Floss?						
Do a wee?						
Take a selfie?						

Total score

PLAYER 1

How much time does your partner spend per day...

	More than 3 hours	2–3 hours	1–2 hours	Less than an hour	No time	Correct? Y=1 N=0
Grooming?						
Watching TV?						
Working?						
Shopping (including online)?						

Total score

PLAYER 2

How much time does your partner spend per day...

	More than 3 hours	2–3 hours	1–2 hours	Less than an hour	No time	Correct? Y=1 N=0
Working out?						
Cleaning/tidying?						
Eating?						
On their phone?						

Total score

PLAYER 1

When was the last time your partner...

	In the past week	In the past month	In the past 6 months	In the past year	Never	Correct? Y=1 N=0
Bought you a gift?						
Bought themselves a gift?						
Arranged a weekend away?						
Cooked you a romantic meal?						

Total score

PLAYER 2

When was the last time your partner...

	In the past week	In the past month	In the past 6 months	In the past year	Never	Correct? Y=1 N=0
Surprised you?						
Took you out for dinner?						
Went out without you?						
Let you choose a movie to watch together?						

Total score

PLAYER 1

How many times has your partner...

	Never	Once	2–5 times	6–10 times	More than 10 times	Correct? Y=1 N=0
Taken their driving test?						
Been in a serious relationship?						
Changed jobs?						
Deleted your number?						

Total score

PLAYER 2

How many times has your partner...

	Never	Once	2–5 times	6–10 times	More than 10 times	Correct? Y=1 N=0
Been in a physical fight?						
Kissed a co-worker?						
Lived with a partner?						
Deleted you off their social media?						

Total score

PLAYER 1

What time of day is your partner at their...

	Early morning	Late morning	Middle of the day	Afternoon to evening	At night	Correct? Y=1 N=0
Most annoying?						
Most hungry?						
Most sexual?						
Most talkative?						

Total score

What time of day is your partner at their...

	Early morning	Late morning	Middle of the day	Afternoon to evening	At night	Correct? Y=1 N=0
Most grumpy?						
Most sociable?						
Most productive?						
Most distracted?						

Total score:

WOULD THEY

RATHER...?

You're mainly used to seeing your partner lounging on the sofa, snuggling in the bed or munching their way through an entire packet of biscuits. But how would they react in more extreme scenarios? What choices would they make if push finally came to shove? In this chapter, you'll be selecting your partner's preferences for some pretty strange stuff.

SCORING SYSTEM

For each question, tick the answer you think your partner would be most likely to choose. Switch players for each question (note: it says Player 1 or Player 2 at the top of each to keep track). At the end of the chapter, give your partner a point if they picked the answer you would have chosen. Whoever has the most points wins.

PLAYER 1

Would your partner rather...?

Correct?
Y=1, N=0

Tick One

Swim with dolphins ☐

Swim with sharks ☐

☐

Ride the Ferris wheel ☐

Ride the roller coaster ☐

☐

Drive-thru McDonald's ☐

Drive past McDonald's ☐

☐

Marry in Vegas ☐

Win in Vegas ☐

☐

Player 1's total score: ☐ /4

PLAYER 2

Would your partner rather...?

Correct?
Y=1, N=0

Tick One

Buy a boat ☐

Build a boat ☐ ☐

Eat cheese ☐

Say cheese ☐ ☐

Always be alone ☐

Always be with people ☐ ☐

Have sex on the beach ☐

Have sex on a bouncy castle ☐ ☐

Player 2's total score: ☐ /4

PLAYER 1

Would your
partner rather...?

Correct?
Y=1, N=0

Tick One

Work hard for more money

Hardly work for less money

Live without the internet

Live without hot water

Be able to teleport

Be able to read minds

Be naked in front of
their boss

See their boss naked

Player 1's total score: ___ /4

PLAYER 2

Would your
partner rather...?

Correct?
Y=1, N=0

Tick One

Climb Mount Everest

Visit the Mariana Trench

Ask a friend for help

Ask a stranger for help

Be a dog

Be a cat

Eradicate war

Eradicate global warming

Player 2's total score: ⬜ /4

PLAYER 1

Would your partner rather...?

Correct?
Y=1, N=0

Tick One

Live on the moon but
never come back to earth ☐

☐

Live on earth but
never go to the moon ☐

Become a robot ☐

☐

Be taken over by robots ☐

Only feel cold ☐

☐

Only feel warm ☐

Join a cult ☐

☐

Start a cult ☐

Player 1's total score: ☐ /4

PLAYER 2

Would your
partner rather...?

Correct?
Y=1, N=0

Tick One

Burn their books ☐

Burn their clothes ☐

☐

Start a new company ☐

Join a touring company ☐

☐

Kill the zombies ☐

Run from the zombies ☐

☐

Live for the moment
and die young ☐

Live a simple life and die old ☐

☐

Player 2's total score: ☐ /4

PLAYER 1

Would your
partner rather...?

Correct?
Y=1, N=0

Tick One

Be funny

☐

☐

Be smart

☐

Travel to the past

☐

☐

Travel to the future

☐

Have super strength

☐

☐

Have super speed

☐

Find out what happens
when you die

☐

☐

Find out if aliens exist

☐

Player 1's total score:

☐ /4

PLAYER 2

Would your
partner...?

Correct?
Y=1, N=0

Tick One

Get rich by luck

Get rich by hard work

You dated their best friend

You dated their arch-enemy

Have free coffee

Have free WiFi

Live in the Harry Potter universe

Live in the Star Wars universe

Player 2's total score: /4

PLAYER 1

Would your partner rather...?

Correct?
Y=1, N=0

Tick One

Get paid for sex ☐

Pay someone else for sex ☐

☐

Have a foot-long nose ☐

Have a foot-long tongue ☐

☐

Have dinner with Kanye West ☐

Have dinner with Donald Trump ☐

☐

Everyone could hear
all their thoughts ☐

☐

They could hear everyone
else's thoughts ☐

Player 1's total score: ☐ /4

PLAYER 2

Would your partner rather...?

Correct?
Y=1, N=0

Tick One

Lose their sight ☐ ☐

Lose their voice ☐

Have no hair ☐ ☐

Have hair all over ☐

Pee him/herself ☐ ☐

Pee on you ☐

Have a head the size of a tennis ball ☐

Have a head the size of a watermelon ☐ ☐

Player 2's total score: ☐ /4

THE ART OF
LOVE

Your partner might look like a work of art, but that doesn't mean you'll find it easy capturing their beauty on paper. For this chapter, you must rely on your inner Van Gogh to draw your partner, their body parts and their favourite things. Pencils (or other artistic media) at the ready...

SCORING SYSTEM

After you've both taken on each drawing challenge, score each other's masterpieces out of 10. If neither of you are talented artists, why not give points for creativity, humour, accuracy, or ridiculousness. At the end of the chapter, add up your points to see who wins the round. If you don't want to see each other's drawings until after you've completed the whole chapter, cover them with a piece of paper as you go along.

PLAYER 1

Draw your partner's sex face:

Player 1's total score: ⬜ /10

PLAYER 2

Draw your partner's sex face:

Player 2's total score: ☐ /10

PLAYER 1

Draw your partner's dream plate of food:

Player 1's total score: [   ] /10

PLAYER 2

Draw your partner's dream plate of food:

Player 2's total score: ☐ /10

PLAYER 1

Draw your partner's favourite sex toy:

Player 1's total score: ☐ /10

PLAYER 2

Draw your partner's favourite sex toy:

Player 2's total score: /10

PLAYER 1

Draw your partner as a superhero:

Player 1's total score: [   ] /10

PLAYER 2

Draw your partner as a superhero:

Player 2's total score: ___ /10

PLAYER 1

Draw your partner's most embarrassing experience:

Player 1's total score: [ ] /10

PLAYER 2

Draw your partner's most embarrassing experience:

Player 2's total score: ___ /10

PLAYER 1

Draw your partner's dream house:

Player 1's total score: ⬜ /10

PLAYER 2

Draw your partner's dream house:

Player 2's total score: _____ /10

PLAYER 1

Draw your partner as an animal:

Player 1's total score: ____ /10

PLAYER 2

Draw your partner as an animal:

Player 2's total score: [   ] /10

RESULTS:
AND THE WINNER IS...

Well done on getting this far without any blood spilled. If you've been writing down your scores for each round, then it's time to add up all your points to see which of you knows the most about the other. If it's you, you can then claim to be the Champion Lover, Relationship Expert, All-Knowing Great One, or whatever other arbitrary title you like.

THE SCORES

Round	Player 1	Player 2
1		
2		
3		
4		
5		
6		
7		
8		
9		
Total		

PREDICTABLE

BEHAVIOUR

When you've known someone for a while (especially if you live with them), you start to learn all the little quirks, tics and bizarre behaviours that make them who they are. In this bonus round, you'll need to channel your partner in order to predict what they would do.

SCORING SYSTEM

For each question, select A, B, C or D. Once you've completed the chapter, add up how many of each letter you picked for your partner. Turn to page 127 to find out what your answers say about the person you're with.

There's a pile of dirty dishes in the sink. Does your partner...

a) Wash them up because you cooked dinner?

b) Wash them up, but not till tomorrow?

c) Tell you it's your turn to do the washing up, even though it's not?

d) Refuse to do them and start browsing dishwashers online?

Player 1: ☐   Player 2: ☐

The shower needs fixing. Is your partner most likely to...

a) Fix it straight away because they're really handy?

b) Phone someone up and pay to get the job done?

c) Leave it for a few weeks like you? You're both as lazy as each other.

d) Do nothing? They know that you will sort it eventually.

Player 1: ☐   Player 2: ☐

You're rushing out the door to work, leaving your partner in bed (they have a day off). When you return home, is your partner most likely to have...

a) Cleaned the house from top to bottom and cooked a romantic dinner?

b) Vacuumed and put a pizza in the oven?

c) Tidied the bed? The place is exactly as you left it.

d) Not got out of bed until you're back to ask you what's for dinner?

Player 1: ☐   Player 2: ☐

Your flight's delayed coming back from holiday. Does your partner...

a) Take you away for another few nights? You might as well make the most of the trip.

b) Plan a fun night in the airport?

c) Spend the evening complaining about the lack of complimentary snacks?

d) Cause a scene, shouting at the airport staff?

Player 1: ☐   Player 2: ☐

Your partner says they're going to the pub for a few drinks after work. What happens next?

a) They're home for dinner and in the mood for love.

b) They saunter in a few hours later.

c) You wake up the next day and find them hungover on the sofa.

d) You find them the following morning asleep in the garden, covered in their own puke.

Player 1: ☐   Player 2: ☐

You go out for dinner to a cool new restaurant, but when you arrive there's a long wait for a table and you're starving. Does your partner...

a) Use their charm to get you seated pronto?

b) Suggest you go somewhere else? They're not bothered either way.

c) Say you should wait it out, but then fail to keep you entertained in the queue?

d) Cause an argument and storm off?

Player 1: ☐   **Player 2:** ☐

You leave the holiday plans up to your partner. Do they book...

a) A luxurious romantic break?

b) A budget break somewhere nice?

c) A weekend at their parents' house?

d) A weekend away with their mates (without you)?

Player 1: ☐   **Player 2:** ☐

Your partner has promised to cook tonight. When you arrive, hungry and ready to eat...

a) There's a delicious meal, wine and candles on the table.

b) You are given beans on toast again.

c) They open the takeaway app on their phone and ask you what you want.

d) They're not home – they've gone to meet a friend.

Player 1: ☐   **Player 2:** ☐

Your partner invites you along to a work event. When you arrive...

a) Everyone's excited to see you – you've met them all before.

b) Your partner makes an effort to introduce you but then talks a lot about work.

c) You spend most of the night with strangers while your partner gets drunk with their friends.

d) You don't see your partner till the next morning – they forgot to invite you to the after party.

Player 1: ☐   **Player 2:** ☐

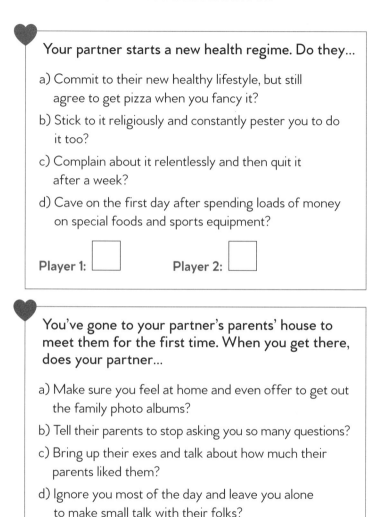

Your partner starts a new health regime. Do they...

a) Commit to their new healthy lifestyle, but still agree to get pizza when you fancy it?

b) Stick to it religiously and constantly pester you to do it too?

c) Complain about it relentlessly and then quit it after a week?

d) Cave on the first day after spending loads of money on special foods and sports equipment?

Player 1: ☐   **Player 2:** ☐

You've gone to your partner's parents' house to meet them for the first time. When you get there, does your partner...

a) Make sure you feel at home and even offer to get out the family photo albums?

b) Tell their parents to stop asking you so many questions?

c) Bring up their exes and talk about how much their parents liked them?

d) Ignore you most of the day and leave you alone to make small talk with their folks?

Player 1: ☐   **Player 2:** ☐

Your partner gets a small bonus from work.
What do they do with the money?

a) They take you away for a romantic weekend break.

b) They take you out for dinner and spend the rest
on stuff just for them.

c) They save it, of course.

d) They have a major shopping splurge, and then ask to
borrow money from you the following weekend.

Player 1: ☐   Player 2: ☐

Your partner goes on a hen/stag weekend away.
What happens next?

a) They come back early because they're missing
you too much.

b) They message you once and then get on with
having fun with their friends.

c) They send you drunk texts all weekend and you see
photos of them gyrating with strangers on social media.

d) You don't hear anything and find out from one of
their friends they've been arrested for drunk and
disorderly behaviour.

Player 1: ☐   Player 2: ☐

You tell your partner a really embarrassing secret about yourself. Do they...

a) Take it to the grave?

b) Tell their closest friend who swears to secrecy?

c) Blurt it out at the pub in front of everyone, hoping you'll see the funny side?

d) Broadcast it on social media minutes after you've told them? It's too shocking/hilarious/mortifying to keep to themselves.

Player 1: ☐　　　Player 2: ☐

Your favourite TV show has just released a new series on Netflix, but you're away on holiday, so you make your partner promise to wait for your return to watch it. Do they...

a) Keep their promise?

b) Watch the first episode, tell you sheepishly and then rewatch it with you when you're back?

c) Watch the entire series, pretend they haven't and then spend the entire time looking at their phone when they have to re-watch it with you?

d) Watch the entire series and then spoil it for you by tweeting about all the plot twists?

Player 1: ☐　　　Player 2: ☐

You buy your partner a present that they don't like/want/need. Do they...

a) Pretend to love it and use it anyway? They wouldn't want to hurt your feelings.

b) Tell the truth and ask to return it?

c) Sell it on eBay without telling you and use the money for something they really want?

d) Start a fight with you about it and make you buy them something else?

Player 1: ☐   Player 2: ☐

Your partner comes down with a cold. What happens next?

a) They suck it up and carry on like normal – it's just a little cold.

b) They take a day off work and catch up on some binge-watching.

c) They complain for a few days and ask you to make them some soup.

d) They lounge on the sofa for a week, whinging constantly, and you have to wait on them, hand and foot.

Player 1: ☐   Player 2: ☐

Your partner plans a surprise date for your birthday. Is it...

a) A perfect (and very organized) day doing what you love.

b) A romantic day with a few mishaps but lots of fun.

c) Dinner at a restaurant you both like but always go to.

d) A day doing something they love. In other words, your idea of hell.

Player 1: ☐   Player 2: ☐

THE SCORES

You've made it! Congratulations on finishing the game – hopefully you're both still smiling and the competition hasn't caused an irreparable rift in your relationship. You already know who the better (half) listener is, but now it's time to find out what you really think of each other. Add up the number of As, Bs, Cs, and Ds you scored each other, and then read on to discover what your answers say you think about your beloved.

Mostly As

You think your partner's the best of the best. They always push the boat out to show you how much they love you, even if it's sometimes a little overkill. Their only fault? They're so goddamn perfect they make you look bad.

Mostly Bs

You think your partner's right for you. They make the effort, most of the time, and try their hardest to make you feel special. They're honest and reliable, although sometimes it would be nice if they went that extra mile.

Mostly Cs

You think your partner could do better. As much as you love them, there is some serious room for improvement – they rarely go out of their way to help out or surprise you, and if they do, it's usually a disaster.

Mostly Ds

You think your partner could soon be your ex. They're selfish and stingy – romance is a concept they've yet to grasp. They'll need to do some serious work to get back in your good books, if it's even possible.

If you're interested in finding out more
about our books, find us on Facebook
at Summersdale Publishers and follow
us on Twitter at @Summersdale.

www.summersdale.com